A1

I began writing scribbles on a piece of notebook paper at a very early age. I was convinced that my immigrant grandmother would believe that I could write a four page journal within a matter of seconds. In a failed attempt, I eventually mustered up the courage to showcase a legitimate piece of my work. With positive reinforcement and a willing family, I was published in a coffee-table book in 2012. With an accumulation of six published works and several other admirable works stored in the folders of my laptop, the idea of publishing a book of my own didn't seem so unrealistic anymore. No longer would I be brandishing scribbles in a faulty diary notebook.

In the year of 2015, three years in the making, "Fluorescent Adolescent" has reached your eyes. Following this very page are a combination of some of my more emotional nights, relinquished spiritual guidance, and proudest moments summed into an anthology for you. The purpose is not to selfishly waver my name on a book. No, that would devalue my words. My mission is to inspire teenagers and the younger generations to embark on a journey that may seem somewhat intangible at first, but all the more accomplishable with time.

Table of Contents

90210 Oligopoly..Page 5

A Drunken Love..Page 6

Beauty and the Beast...Page 7

Constellations..Page 8

Drowning For You..Page 9

I Don't Enjoy...Page 10

I Fell In Lust...Page 12

Irremovable Stains..Page 13

Letting Go..Page 14

Milky Way..Page 15

My Crystal Cove...Page 16

My Green House...Page 17

My Heart's Resignation.....................................Page 18

My Memory..Page 19

My Once Hollow Bones.....................................Page 20

Nocturnal Thoughts..Page 21

Painful Progression...Page 22

Salted Scars...Page 23

The Beauty in Women......................................Page 24

The Heavenly Bird..Page 26

The Irony in Society...Page 28

The Justified Potentiality..........................Page 29

The Last Winter...Page 30

The Satisfaction in Dying..........................Page 32

Jump Over This Blinking Cursor................Page 33

What a Masterpiece.................................Page 34

What You've Done....................................Page 36

Your Dummy...Page 38

The Web of a Broken Future.....................Page 39

Heavy Conscience....................................Page 40

Tranquility in Old Age...............................Page 41

Female Adoration.....................................Page 42

The Expanding Female Generation...........Page 43

To My Future Daughter............................Page 45

Happy Halloween.....................................Page 48

The Unruly Aftermath..............................Page 49

After Reaching Your Dreams....................Page 51

Walk a Mile in His Shoes..........................Page 52

Tribute to In-N-Out..................................Page 53

Revelation of Me......................................Page 54

The End of Time.......................................Page 55

The Beginning of Something Greater........Page 56

The Shape of Love....................................Page 57

Priceless Art..Page 58

The Side Effects of Dreaming......................Page 59

Table for One...Page 60

Spring Cleaning..Page 61

The Game..Page 62

90210 Oligopoly

Beauty has been shaped
by a societal thought
molded to shape us
into something we are not.

So why is it,
I ask you,
do we continue to follow
the 90210 oligopoly
keeping our insides hollow.

A Drunken Love

He was what she needed,
the feeling of drunkenness –
iced liquor to her dreams awaiting her reality.
An introduction to the oblivion side deceived her every limb of passion,
the jagged love to who she was, the residency within her.
She needed to believe it could be so easy.
The warmth and the comfort –
what, before, she felt unwillingly.
She needed to feel resentment,
regret towards never having kept what was promising,
what was innocent and naïve,
what was pure and honest,
She had to learn from a drunken love the way he learned from her.
She had to taste something intolerable the way he used her.
"Lie to me again," she murmured.
He whispered, "I love you."

Beauty and the Beast

The limit of tolerance has grown its veins past the brink of my skin.
Bones cracking and breaking have formed this new being I can't seem to understand.
It has indefinitely poured its emotions and heavy burdens blatantly on my once so angelic and care-free face.
It has taken a toll on my sanity and reality causing havoc in my heart and my brain
pushing past the bones and walls which cover them up so neatly
only to reveal my thoughts which I've devised to hide so intently.
I've only come to realize that this beast has come from inside
revealing a truth I have never seemed to even want to acknowledge.
Reaching an age when the urge to need,
and want,
and feel
has reached the breaking point past the desperation
of just a separate hand and body
none other than the other half of my soul.
The beast reclines back inside my brain and my heart.
My bones crawl their way back to their original form as my skin mends together
to form a porcelain doll which only shines in the light of the forsaken audience
that has only jailed me behind these shiny, plastic walls.
Forevermore waiting for the next curtain call to play a one man show of
beauty and the beast.

Constellations

And for the longest time she laid there in silence,
counting the stars.
She came across a falling star
and that's when she realized
not even a falling star
could save her anymore.

Drowning For You

The waves, so blue and green, take me away,
washing my body helplessly further in towards the sunset where I
see a brighter side.
An innocent warmth that just feels so pure soothes every inch of my
helpless body.
I duck my head into the warmth of you
feeling the rough seaweed touch my lips,
my arms,
my hands,
my cheeks.
Suddenly, what was once my greatest nightmare has turned into
my never-before dream.
My body twirls and flows into your heart ever more.
I am falling for your waves
realizing nothing on this earth
can ever possibly take me away.

I Don't Enjoy

I don't enjoy the feeling of not being loved in return...
I don't enjoy how when I look earnestly in your eyes, I receive a state of complete sobriety
as if our reality has wiped the remainder of tequila and beer from your lips.
I don't enjoy dancing with a partner that only remains idle during the moments I've needed to dance the most
just to keep me happy and sane that much longer..
I don't see that you enjoy me and I don't see you stumbling over your toes in a hurry
to welcome me with an embrace I've grown to take advantage of.
I smell the same love I've wanted since the day we first started dancing
but it feels like this song has grown old for you
and you've just begun looking for another tune.
While I am trying to fill the steps your feet followed,
trying to remember the way the warmth of your body leaned against mine,
I'm wondering if I'm the only one left dancing and when I will get over this tune too.
I've familiarized myself with salted rims and alcohol shots
that can never seem to substitute the taste of your lips.
And all this has taken me back to your drunken toes falling over another
and I wonder if you meant to tell me you felt like this on your way to dancing another tune with me...

I'm sorry I could never get the steps right and that I only remained
stepping on your toes
but your smile has engraved itself on the waves of my brain and I
can't seem to understand
that you have chosen to forget me as you would forget an old song.
You've tuned me out and neglected my needs
and selfishly I am blaming alcohol on the death of us
but how could I blame what only began the birth of us.
You kissed me today and your lips tasted of sharp, pungent mint…
as if you've washed out my taste and our wrecked love of alcohol
only to substitute it
with a mature image and perception of something we refused to
submit to…

I Fell In Lust

I fell in love with the way you glazed my hipbone
just as your eyes began to open
from the late midnight conversations
passionate words messaged back and forth.

I fell in love again
when you finally opened your eyes –
exchanging lazy morning smiles
as our limbs stretched for air
under the white cloud covers
yearning for warmth,
crawling back to one another.

I fell in love again on our way to the coffee shop.
The way you wore two different socks and your hair going every
which way,
the way you ordered a coffee with two sugars
when you really meant three,
using milk in your coffee
when you really meant cream.

Looking down at my hand
exchanged love notes written on our palms
was when I realized I fell in lust.
In lust with your presence,
in lust with your words.
But I realized I had not fallen in love with you.

Irremovable Stains

Coffee stained her teeth
and smoldered her tongue
as she choked on a cupful
in hope that it would somehow
wake every single cell of her body
from the tormenting dreams
that never failed to welcome her
in her every slumber;
Blotting the stain
the way her memories grew a pain --
just more hopefully
yet less noticeably.
Gust of wind caressed her skin
and lulled her with muffled melody
as she embraced the breeze
that greeted her with relish
as if it understood her undying misery
that she concealed imperfectly
from everyone she knew
desiring that eventually she'd get through.

Letting Go

I've learned to let go.
I've learned that at times
it is during our free fall that we begin to understand everything
we've taken for granted.
I've learned that through our greatest demise
we find a reason to prevail.
It is only during those moments that we take pride in who we've
become.
Forevermore welcome life's greatest turmoil.
You will learn your weaknesses,
recognize your strengths,
and learn more about yourself in those few days,
hours,
minutes,
or even seconds
than you have learned in your entire human existence.

Milky Way

Into the windows of your soul
through the glistening reflection
of your two beautifully unwritten eyes,
the stars of the Milky Way align to remind me
"This isn't the end,"
and, "You'll be okay."
Your eyes have shown me
the unrecognized souls in the midnight sky..
which remind me every day that
there is more to life beyond my own self-indulgent surmise.

My Crystal Cove

The burrows of my heart have been packed with ceaseless energy from harvests prior.
And I've gone through cleaning what has been packed so tightly, shedding tears over pictures I hadn't seen from years ago
and exchanged love notes signed by the dates in which you wrote them to me –
A time when forever was a possibility and you weren't so far away.
I begin to push the pictures back into the crevices in which I found them.
Cleaning them out would only create more empty spaces.
I've found that if I forget you
I can't show someone else my history.
I want to give someone a fighting chance to show me better than what used to be.
I think I deserve to know what love can truly mean.

My Green House

I tried to stop loving you
but you grew roots around my ribcage,
the place I call home,
and you sprouted flowers just below my collarbones.
Just as you smile
the sun smiles with you and you curve in my direction.
Just then I find myself captivated,
intoxicated by your smell,
inspired by your roots,
in need of your touch,
thorns and all.
An addiction to you,
a need for you.
And even though I pluck your petals
trying to resist your poison,
I have not yet figured out why I cannot stop loving you.

My Heart's Resignation

The clouds start to hover
as dreamt thoughts take over,
and the waves roll under
as shortage of breath cuts shorter.

The droplets of rain are covered by the tidings of the waves,
but the disappointment is seen by the hovering of the clouds
resembling that heavy feeling in that unbroken chest,
that sheer humiliation,
and that pure disappointment --
They all led unto my heart's permanent resignation.

My Memory

Your lips have pressed mine enough now
that they have left a print forever on my heart.
My nose lured in by a comforting bounty
tied together by a warm embrace.
Your eyes will stare back at mine –
emotions and passion, pages folding one after another,
whilst I follow your every move.
And all that time, I was only hoping with all my soul
that you would never be just a memory.

My Once Hollow Bones

My hollow bones have now been filled with the overwhelming
waves of your love
that have left me idling back and forth between complete insanity
and mindless reality.
All the same, these two ideas grow to intertwine as our fingers have
learned to find a home within each other's pulse,
clinging back to what we
believe is safety.
So completely naive I have grown in your sunlit daze that I have
forgotten
what I will ever become when I reach the day to find that
you are not around.
I've been laying on my arm for quite some time
and my pulsating veins have seemed to shaken my torso rocking me
back and forth.
And as I begin to feel the buzzing sensation across my limbs,
numbing my every nerve,
the thought of you comes to mind and I can't help but to smile at
the mere thought
of no longer being in control.

Nocturnal Thoughts

Abstract emotions
cause the greatest havoc
rising questions of insanity
and ethics or morality.

How do my limbs remain still
while my mind runs wild with slumber imagination.
What is it that even our thoughts
cannot control what we most desire.

In my efforts to remain nocturnal
and only sleep when my rest is in jeopardy,
I sleep like a bat
clenching onto everything around me.

Bony limbs of hallow decor
and wings to cover the moon light,
I grasp hold of my reality
until I soon realize
even nightly bats who sleep so solemnly subdued
must sleep with their world upside down
controlled by abstract emotions:
Governed by no one
and felt by everyone.

Painful Progression

I've been striving for independence too long
to understand that maybe it's not enough.
Maybe I've been lopsided for quite some time
applying too much pressure to a wound I never had
which has left me bruised and sore in a place
I never thought I had a problem.

It wasn't until I lifted the gauze did I realize
that the rubbing alcohol had run out
and that I had been covering something
that has now grown to surpass the blockade
of this 4x4 cotton swab...

My pride has forced me to deny that this was all my fault
and that I can easily go onto change who I am and how I pursue,
but how will I ever hide the thing that makes me so ugly,
so inconceivably horrid to even imagine...
How do I change what I believed
had been so familiar to me
for countless years...

Now that the blood has trickled down several different paths
a few adjoining with others
I wonder when my path will follow with another...
And I wonder when I will be able look down at progression
and not see pain and resentment...

Salted Scars

Words never satisfy your longing for change
I cannot keep you away from anything beyond me.
My warmth has grown cold from being deserted during my coldest demise.
My only heat source was you.
And since you've gone, my lips remain frozen.
My ligaments refuse to bend and my salted wounds will not close.
You've re-opened my scars and left me to question forever more.

Like the shore which kisses the ground you once walked on,
I will forever return to your feet in utter humility.
I will always come back to you.
However, I am afraid the ozone is melting
and I cannot stop my heart from overbearing.
I've tried to let you free,
but my heart will not let me.
Do not question why I dry you out or only sting the wounds
someone else created for you.

Although I return,
I depart from your feet every second.
And like the ocean
I will only wash away your worries whenever you come back to me.
But do not wonder why it burns to close your new wounds.
I'll be sure to leave scars in remembrance of the way you've abandoned me.

The Beauty in Women

It is only natural to compare a waist size with another
and wish for a few less inches to match with those slender hips
before your eyes.
It is only natural to compare a skin tone with another
only a few more minutes in the sun and you'd be the perfect bronze
gold
your eyes only wish to become.
It is only natural to compare a hair style with another
wishing some curls would go the way you wanted them to
and the straw like frizz one step above your actual head
would agree with the weather of the day
just once.

But ladies,
it is just as natural to cherish youthful hips,
or a body that has mothered
just as much as it is natural to understand that priorities and life
come in first
while perfect curls and tanned skin
come in last.
And with every flaw and every undesirable trait
you so wish you could erase from your body
your mother once traced with her very fingers
promising to always love and cherish every inch you choose to
betray,
your father intended to keep hidden
so that no other person could take his little princess away from him,

your future lover combined so expertly
waiting for the day to meet someone just like you,
your spouse falls in a sweet lullaby of pure innocence,
dreaming of the way your perfections make him or her smile each
and every day.
It is only natural to wish to be everything you're not,
and never understand the true sentiment of rare beauty.
But understand that what you see,
may be a mile long shot from what others have already understood.

The Heavenly Bird

At the age of one day I was set out on a porch.
To my parents there was no other way,
they gave me to a man by the name of George.
George had red hair with dark brown eyes
and skin oh so fair, with him, I would arise.
He never came out much for he was a man of few words.
He walked with a crutch. It was hard to walk forward.
He gave me the best that he could -- A father to call my own.
His fatigue, I understood. Each day we both had grown.
I helped him walk, he helped me read, he helped me talk, to help
each other we agreed.
One night I could not sleep for a bird was persistently chirping.
Outside I heard a creek, so I began the lurking.
Oh the bird was so beautiful, mysterious, and light;
My curiosity, as usual, took me out on the night.
I followed the creature from First Street to Seventh.
Examining its every feature, the wonders became my heaven.
I heard a loud bang within the Seventh Street ally.
I tried to make a dash when I soon learned of the rally.
Two men with gang affiliated signs enlaced upon their forearms.
Yes, I screamed and I cried, but no one heard my alarm.
As my vision went bleak and my voice gave up
I suddenly heard a shriek from the old man that grew me up.

With me, he passed from shock and heartache.
The cruelty was harsh and rash, but come and partake.
Those words I screamed I learned from him.

And he learned from me how to run with every limb.
We utilized each other, and that's why we both left.
Never one without the other, and now forever, we are blessed.

The Irony in Society

Oh, the Irony
in an imperfect society
ruled by demented tyranny
demanding perfection mildly.

Until the world sinks
into an everlasting abyss.
Our happiness, society's drink
for what they believe is remiss.

Providing a textbook definition
of what is right and what is wrong
neglecting the pre-k lessons
that the world is something strong.

And that the world is something beautiful
no matter what the case may be.
But inevitably, we are not crucible
and should be treated gently.

Damaging naïve souls.
Terrorizing the lives of the insecure.
Drilling the idea that the world
is defined by a reflection in the mirror.

The Justified Potentiality

How can letter grades
justify the universal understanding
that the infamous letter A
vindicates a failure versus someone outstanding.

And why is it, I wonder,
does the number on a scoreboard
stand as an excuse for the numbers
of hours spent off the court.
Why is talent never seen
and only tested by a percentage
a number, letter, or mien
also known as just a minor appendage.

I realize there is a scale
that all people must abide by
no matter how young or frail,
yet my question still remains why.
Talent is never seen
for it cannot be warranted
by a number or a letter or mien
all draw to a pyramid.

Those who conquer success, I've found,
may not always be an honor roll student graduate.
All the while, the process is still around
severing the talented; the justification, their amputate.

The Last Winter

Remember
that winter
I lost a flower?
The one with white petals,
kind of like a dandelion,
yet soft to the touch
like that of a rose.
Running the years away,
a life of no value
you slipped from my hands.
I looked back at you
and you continued to smile.
You laid on the floor with us.
Naïve brunette curls
bouncing in the wind
giggling and laughing
and you continued to smile.

Remember
the next winter
when I looked back again?
Only this time
I could not find you.
My laughing cut abrupt
and my curls faded away.
My face grew stone cold.
When I finally found you

your petals turned grey,
your thorns grew dull,
and your stems grew into sticks.

Do you still remember
when I picked you up again?
Lost and bewildered
and still very naive
I planted you in the ground.
As several winters passed
my tears became your water,
my sorrow turned into your feed,
my touch became the sun's rays,
and my prayers turned into your gardener.

Another winter passed
and you slivered back into the earth.
The place you grew
was your residency of death.
I will never forget
your smile back at me
and every winter, I promise
to laugh and smile back at you
only to remember
the last winter.

To Uncle Reza

The Satisfaction in Dying

Have I managed to risk it all to fall this far...
Watching a crowd hurry beneath my toes
as my body slowly wavers upon the idea
of going rogue or to forever persevere
I begin to question if I will ever be what you need,
and if I was ever what you wanted.
With due time,
gravity works against my limbs
and my arms which flung heavily by my sides
have been lifted by the air beneath my wings...
I never imagined dying
would ever feel this satisfying.

Jump Over This Blinking Cursor

Watching the cursor
blink rapidly before my eyes
like a tapping foot
nagging my patience,
she balances her petty excuses
on my thin line drawn between
where you are
and where you should be.

And I refuse to believe
you still don't wonder
what it would be like
to kiss me without feeling guilty...
So what's stopping you?

Are you afraid to jump off this colossal cliff
I've grown to show you
how high we could grow.
Do you feel safer
jumping off her hill
only five feet off the ground
so you're sure to stick the landing.

Decide whether you will free fall or never feel the thrill again..
Meanwhile the line grows thicker
and I doubt you'll jump across
that endless abyss.

What a Masterpiece

Sometimes I grow frustrated,
so annoyed we cannot communicate
through words of greatest simplicity
you seem to find hard to verbalize.

Your passion runs deep,
and I'm thankful for learning such a great attribute from you.
But in some ways,
I wish you weren't so strong and opinionated.
I wish you would just listen and learn as I have from you.

For many years you have taught me your lessons on life,
and you have learned a great deal from me as well.
We are two different beings, we are two different women.
We have grown in two different worlds,
that have for better or worse influenced our lives in ways we can
never repay.

Least to say, I am forever grateful for the opportunity you have
given me with this new world.
But my world and my opinions are that of my own.
And respectively, I choose to disagree with most of yours.

All I ever ask of you is to remain open-minded and modest,
humble towards another perspective.
Maybe we are both missing an aspect to the greater picture.
But a masterpiece only remains in pieces until it has been explored,

until it has been so heavily debated and so passionately sketched,
to the point where not a single corner remains meaningless.

The world is our easel and its altercations are our colors.
Let us create a masterpiece with that of the world,
And the two most important pieces –you and me.

To mommy

What You've Done

You've taken a piece of me I will never regain.
You've filled the pages of memories I had planned as a teen.
You've messed me up in such a way
that I replay those moments over and over again
never ceasing to blame myself for letting go of what was once so
close to home.

You've gone away to find another home
in the arms of another woman.
I blamed you for never telling me what really weighed heavy on
your heart until I realized...
It was me.
And ironically in those moments of pure desperation
I tried to run to you and I tried to save you,
but my hands hit a glass wall and you left me without a goodbye.
Your salvation was away from home.

It's been several years
and I continue to look through that glass window
devising the ways to selfishly bring you back to where I believe you
belong.
However, my happiness has now grown acute to the mountainous
measure of your
colossal new world.. Your new home... Your new love...

Forevermore looking through a clear window pane which was a
mere facade of

everything I wanted us to become
blocked by a clear bulletproof glass I could never seem to break no matter how
close I felt to your heart...
My home has left me with all the memories I stitched in it's walls... With videos and photographs we never managed to have time to capture.. It has left me with less I had imagined to gain.. With less than I ever had.. With less of a heart I so passionately shared.. It has left me entirely searching for a reason to ever roam again without my home.

Your Dummy

All your promises have piled up past the brink of my throat.
They've tied together into a knot I can't seem to swallow,
into something I cannot digest,
something I want to forget —
but you won't let me.

Every day
I am reminded of your promises.
And in my brain
your voice plays like a broken record.
My fingers move along with your tune,
and my arms are connected to the strings of your life.

You give me nothing more
than just broken promises
and a life I never had the choice of living.

The Web of a Broken Future

I wonder what it feels like
to have your opinions suffocated
by the straw-like, jagged fingers of the ones we implore...
I wonder what it feels like
to no longer have an identity
as our eyes are forced shut
while our consciences remains alive
crawling out of the lifeless tombs we call humanity
only to have slithered onto somewhere we may never see again...
I wonder what it feels like to have a broken heart...
I wonder if you ever felt second best..
And if your skin still itches from the soul
you took away from my body
the night you dismissed us...
I wonder if like a fly
I was dumb enough to trap myself into your web
as your conniving arms wrapped me
continuously into a web of broken promises...
I wonder how I tasted on your lips...
And I wonder if you left because I just never hit the spot...
I wonder sometimes if there was ever anyone else who found that
spot before I
ever had the chance...

Heavy Conscience

The weight of your gravity
has brought me down.
And I found that I am
a nuisance if I stay around.
I will not desert you
because I made a promise to love you.
However, time has taken over,
and my being has fallen through.
There is a shine in your eye
each time you shed a tear.
Do not mourn my death,
for the galaxy will resolve your fears.
I am still around
just beyond the stellar nebula.
Other stars have been born
from the beautiful death of us.

Tranquility in Old Age

Why is it that when we see the elderly in solidarity,
the strings of our hearts tug at our tears readily strolling down our cheeks..
Are we afraid of being alone..
Are we afraid that we will have no one to accompany us to a simple meal only to ask, "How was your day?"
Are we scared that one day, we will no longer have the support of our mothers and fathers, our friends, and our lovers?
Are we afraid to die, let alone dine alone?
I smile when I see the elderly sitting alone...
They still have a reason to eat and even be... They haven't given up..
As I've grown older and as they probably recognize,
I'm not afraid to be alone..
I'm afraid of never wanting to live anymore.

Female Adoration

Under the curve of her nose
lies the natural sharp lining of her lips
curling up to form a smile
which never fails to radiate any dark room
leaving a warmth unlike any blistering day.
Her eyelids grow acute
as she speaks the name of another man
who will eventually be the reason for why her rotund cheeks of
lilac
flush with artificial wine kisses
that will never deserve even the slight brisk
of her drunken shoulder.
Her porcelain, marble skin
beams with a smile
she has unknowingly taken advantage of --
So much so
that my skin melts with the rays of her presence
while her body and mind remain perfectly statuesque.
Admired by passers-by,
I've grown deprived of sound judgment
for her beauty has muted my sanity.
And I've only been able to watch her perform
a never ending ballet
of silent bliss
of which I could undoubtedly feel
just beneath my fingertips.

The Expanding Female Generation

I am upset with the way we have raised our daughters believing the same excuse,
"It's not that we don't trust you,
we just don't trust the environment."
I don't believe there is any coincidence
that men in the animal kingdom are expected to look after the children
while females search around for the family means.
I don't find it amusing
that women have been the game-changer since they've been recognized
and I most certainly do not find it funny
that you believe I cannot protect myself when my freedom has been jailed
such as that of a lion in captivity who is only yearning for a taste of zebra blood.
It's almost insulting to result to never trusting my environment.
For if I die in a car crash 2 minutes away from home, or days away,
the result is all the same.
Nonetheless however, I can die knowing
that you gave me a chance anyway.
This has turned into a journal rather than the freedom of poetry.
But how can I expect you to understand
when I've been hiding my opinions under my bed instead of
publishing it for the world to see.
I am just as capable as any other man if not more inept and precarious.

Believe that your daughters deserve the option
before you decide to blame uncontrollable fate
as a reason for their barred off parameter.

To My Future Daughter
7 days until the end of the world

1. It's not the end of the world.
Yes, your favorite jeans may have ripped and your artificially straightened hair may have frizzed
and yes, this is the day of school pictures
but understand that with memories snapped behind the lens of invention,
you have the rest of your life for better pictures.

2. It's not the end of the world.
It may look like a boulder in the mirror
and you may have irritated the hill which has now grown into a mountain or more a volcano erupting with puss that you've accumulated through endless squeezing and ceaseless effort to minimize but have only maximized, but give it time.
Time is all you need to heal anything.

3. It's not the end of the world.
Unforgiven rumors that have slipped through your lips may have tainted a friendship you thought would've lasted and you would've depended on for the nights of tears and maybe even pointless laughter and slumber parties talking about boys infested with cooties and how they will never come between you and their friendship.
But anything good must come to an end and understand that every friend has a limit and every person has a flaw but not every person

is secure and you will too learn that with every message in a bottle, there is a consequence to opening to cork.

4. It's not the end of the world.

I may not understand your emotions and what you're going through, but give me time and give me patience and I will learn to understand your language. I will promise to give you time and give you my patience to understand that my daughter comes before work, and before friends, and sometimes even before my husband because your happiness is mine and what am I without you, right?

5. It's not the end of the world.

They don't see all that you are in my eyes. I know I'm just your mom and I am expected to put you on a pedestal, but you really are indescribably beautiful and I wish for the day for you to meet someone who makes you feel more alive than I ever could and makes you believe meaningless phrases I have voiced with a dying plea hoping you will eventually trust me when I tell you …

6. It's not the end of the world.

He may have told you he loved you, and he may have promised to have given you everything, and in return you may have believed that you could trust him. But didn't mommy ever tell you the only people you can trust in life is that of your own family? Why didn't you trust the womb that brought you into this world and instead choose to trust the conniving monster that tricked you into believing that he was a far better risk than I was?

7. It's not the end of the world.

It may have been a long night of tears and you may have not eaten anything to fill the belly that will eventually carry your own daughter after the grains of your future have been flung over your head, but understand that I am here to understand and I am not your worst enemy so you can trust me. I will not hurt you. I will not desert you. I will be your mommy even when you've left this house and married the man who finally meant those three words and promised you a life full of happiness and effort to be forever yours.

8. It's not the end of the world.

You must understand that like any other corpse, mine will eventually die. Everybody has a timeline, and a due date, and unfortunately, mine has come around sooner than you expected. But understand that I have been avoiding ever witnessing this pain you feel in the pit of your belly and the tug of your heart strings. I'm sorry that I can't be there to wipe away your tears... but please understand that this day is not the end of the world. It is the beginning of a new world which revolves around the body of your daughter that I hope you will indubitably caution from the 7 days until the end of her world.

Happy Halloween

Move into my body
and decorate my organs with love
and detrimentally heart shattering sincerity.
Pick up the broken pieces and dump them into your box of candies
overflowing with Snickers and Twix and my favorite, white
chocolate kisses reminding me of the way your cracked lips spread
in an array of lines panned together like bat wings which smile so
flirtatiously back at my gaze that I can never seem to break.
Disperse pieces of my love for everyone to see that I am really not
that crazy.
That you've burst open my pretentious gingerbread walls topped
with icing and stale corn candy that no one ever eats on Halloween
which has shamelessly allowed me to share with others this
overbearing love I have only just begun to share.
Wear my spleen as your costume
and erase the cobwebs from the veins of my newly pumping heart
that has only begun to live and love for you.
Adorn my imperfections across the front porch for everyone to see
and scare away the trick-or-treaters from your guilty pleasure with
the only thing no one will ever be able to buy around Halloween –
the horrifying beauty you see in me.

The Unruly Aftermath

You've left a mess of my body and mind spread across a granite floor that I have managed to lose grip of knowing you've opened up my heart like an oil tank and labelled my remains as "toxic waste," only to caution others from ever entering a place only YOU could never handle.

See, I knew you didn't have the means to support my colossal dreams but I replaced my pillow of dreams with the lifelines of your palms artificially carved with doubtful screams I heard each time I laid my head down onto empty hands that always remained freezing.

I began to wonder if you were ever human. If, when you chose me, you had planned to take away my sincerity to selfishly humanize the robot I've never failed to refill every night with streams of salted water rolling down my cheeks only to remind me of the control I gave you to undermine me.

I guess my emotions rusted away at you too much one night. You opened up my wounds and used the oil within me to smooth out your once rusted limbs to leave me trickling until the very last drop.

See, you never closed me.

I should've known you were careless of school, our future, and my heart. But I never thought you'd blame another man who has humbly worn the fluorescent orange vest mopping away at the grimy remains you've filled within me only to empty, selflessly assuming responsibility for your insincerity. Please remind me of a time a ruler came back into power to assume his righteous position to govern his country only to break it down once again and move onto the ruins of my insecurities you were well aware of.

You've deserted monuments that have been recoiled and rebuilt by the hands of another man and you have the nerve to tell me I'm wasteful, that I am undeserving and I am the abuser when my ruins have been left purposeless until I met the hands of divine prosperity.

Don't despise another man for cleaning up the mess you made and never had the tools to clean.

After Reaching Your Dreams

I'm hungry for my discovery
Starving for the only thing that can make me live
In a land of frugality and disparity
I've learned to bargain my way towards a gluttony that has been unsatisfying since the moment I've brought it close to the touch of my lips.
My greatest wishes now taste like poison and stale dreams that have become too easy to reach.
I'm seeking a sweeter reward, a greater meal, it's my survival and I'm not so sure I'm the fittest.
But I'm willing to die for my last meal.

Walk a Mile in His Shoes

Your band aid words have layered heavily on my wounded shoulders
that have been gaping open to reveal my jagged bones etched with another love.
I've begun peeling each Band-Aid off on my own.
Understanding that with time, I've grown and I've healed and this love we had was real but as temporary as your love. Didn't you know I was looking for something worth your weight in gold?
You haven't filled the empty spaces within your steel toed shoes.
You've only kicked at the rocks beneath your feet blaming anyone but yourself.
You've been looking for love on an empty plate,
bandaging the shattered glass together so that it may no longer seep past the shield you've begun to form...
But I like to bleed..
I like the pain I feel after having fallen in love and having it vanish from my own eyes.
You can't protect me forever,
I never asked you to.
I never expected you to fill those shoes...

Tribute to In-N-Out

When I bite into you
the many flavors within you seep past your buns and onto my
tongue
creating this somewhat phallic boner in my mouth as your seeds
slash between my teeth.
The crunch of your stems hit the spot so much more than the
unpreserved mimics of you. Finishing my last bite with a swig of
iced Dream,
I can't imagine an In-N-Out burger getting better than this.

Revelation of Me

Is it a horrible thing to say that the moment I dismissed you
sparked the beginning of my revelation..
My need to conquer something greater.
I'm not saying you're anything but a grand reward.
Know that I once believed this life couldn't possibly be any better
within the grasp of your arms.
But my, oh my, when you let me go...
It seemed as though your arms weighed two tons each
and my forearms were unable to understand the difference
between a cage and sincerity.
I'm still trying to figure out which one you were.

I know your motives were unintentional and subconsciously I knew
what I was getting into when I decided to call you mine.
I just never took into account that I would be yours –
My mind,
my soul,
my body.
Everything had the label of your initials that later on turned into a
whole heart that has made me stronger than I was before.
I don't regret having met you. I don't resent you.
I cherish you for allowing me to realize that I'm not ready to be
confined.
That I have much more to see,
much more to learn,
much more to conquer.

The End of Time

I am afraid I don't have enough time to reach my full potential.
I'm afraid of the excuses that have found homes
in the darkest, deepest concave burrows of my malnourished
dreams.
I'm afraid that fear will be the death of me.
And by that time, I'm afraid that my burial will begin with the
words of fear
that severed the things I never had enough time to conquer.
I'm afraid to say there will be a day I will no longer be afraid.
Rather I will be too old and it will be too late
to be me in my entirety.

The Beginning of Something Greater

I've begun to question the menial impact I have on this world.
I have begun to undermine my ability as a woman to be the walking role model for younger generations.
I have only begun to realize that my voice is not global and my words are not universal. However, my actions are my survival that will one day save another misunderstood girl.
I have only begun to understand the footprint I leave behind each time the eyes of youth idol at my complexion.
I will cup those cheeks of admiration and look behind the eyes of envy to tell the girls of our expanding feminist culture that behind our eyelids of artificial painting and dreams locked behind the film of skin which close our eyes each and every night...
That our dreams are tangible and our eyelids may close on us from our dreams.
But the very morning we awake to our reality is the day to understand our journey has just begun.
And we must embark on our dreams in a last attempt to even survive.
We are the women, the girls, the unexplainably battered souls of the next generation awaiting our revelation.
Let this not be seen as minuscule.
Maximize your depth and you too will begin to understand that one person can only do so much.
But this is only the beginning.

The Shape of Love

"What's your preferred sex," I've been asked.
I've been left idling with this same perplexed expression on my face.
Would "straight" suffice?
Heterosexual?
Can the person I love but have never met be given a defined term?
Geometry?
Anatomy?
Have we become the generation seeking for answers.
succumbing to meanings handed to us on a piece of paper
generalizing us onto this statistic
dividing us from what really isn't divisible at all!
Honestly, love is love,
whether or not I am seen as straight
is beyond the anatomy of my heart.
I am not two mounds adjoined by two straight lines meeting a sharp corner.
I am just as misunderstood as the very word itself.
Straight?
I am the definition of a hopeless romantic.
Love sees no image. It feels bountiful, it feels beauty.
But most of all, it does not judge us nor does it pin us to a single word only to ease the hearts and minds of the judgmental.

Priceless Art

I've only begun to graffiti my body with quotes and promises I've
made myself.
I've removed and scarred my skin with those bargains I broke.
But I remember them.
I remember them as they are --
Milestones that were simply too far away from the greater picture.
I brandish them,
wear skin tight leather,
only white so that the skin may tarnish every outfit I wear.
I'm too proud to not have anyone look at me and wonder,
"Why doesn't she wear cleaner clothes."
My story is too long for tattoos,
full of many failures that make it almost impossible to hide them
with any other art work.
I fill my walls with my work.
I am my own gallery and my experience is priceless.

The Side Effects of Dreaming

Dreams go
where life fades.
But my life begins
with a grasp of my dream.
Reality brings me down
to where the water lies beneath my knees.
My lips and nose are well above sea level
but my movement is drowning.
I've grasped the turf beneath my feet,
been soiled by the dirt beneath my fingertips.
I've been touched by reality in numerous ways,
I can't even remember a day that I've touched life.
My life is as untouchable as my dreams.
And my future may seem unstable and crazy,
but let life show you crazy behind the film that regenerates behind
your eyelids --
Then you will grow just as crazy as me & believe that dreams are as
attainable as the concrete objects of reality.

Table for One

Do you ever get so bored you entertain your past?
You allow trespassers to reclaim their unreserved seats.
Adorn their table with decorations and table settings,
utensils and napkins folded in an array of shapes.
House-warming party for a body you could never call a home until
just recently.
I've grown isolated from the child I used to know,
awaiting my turn at the big kids' table as my past ghosts haunt the
person I used to be.
How, before, I grew infatuated with the sound of words
but have now become the artist behind their lips.
I've tied my strings to their vocal chords and have allowed myself to
hear what I've longed for years prior.
I'm proud of my manipulation,
of my ingenuity and my new self.
Allowing the past to overcome me is something my child-self
would've allowed.

Spring Cleaning

Clean out my past of any toxins
and replace them with memories of you.
Memories we haven't had
but will only begin to form
with just the touch of your fingers
or your lackadaisical smile;
Help me understand the benefits of a cleanse,
of a detox,
of lessons learned and accepted accompanied by memories that
leave a gaping wound.
I haven't any room for a few more mistakes.
I haven't any room for jokes,
for tales,
for unwarranted memories that inflame the past.
Alleviate these words
with the cause of your liquid courage.
The effects will pay off,
the side effects will benefit you.
My memories are as heavy as they are light.

The Game

Men don't seek love
or seek acceptance in the way women do.
Our actions are done with a purpose,
to be greater than the thought hovered around a man's erection.
I cannot represent all women when I state
that love has become a burden on our hearts.
A table for the party of two
has now left a bird with a broken wing
and one side of the table cleared to make use of empty dishes.
Just so, this bird is left flying in circles
until they begin to realize that this journey has left them with the
same pursuit --
Unsuccessful with no direction.
Only until we have come full circle do we begin to realize
that the heart of men is vicious and unruly.
Do not question my theory or disprove my logic.
This is careful experimentation from many years prior.
I refuse to let my heart go another day
flying in the same circle
with the hope that a man will treat me well
with the intention of just being a decent human being,
with the intention of allowing my trust to not be broken,
with the intention of not soiling my love by intermingling it with a
love not so deserving.
There is simply no love in a man's eyes that has already tasted its
reward,
its prize.

I've allowed the ribbons adorning my hips
slide past my caged heart
and over my neck
welcoming this unanswered question
to sever my mind from my body.
I get it now, I truly do.

Made in the USA
San Bernardino, CA
29 April 2015